Flying with Fear

Flying with Fear

My journey across the world

by Elizabeth Bond

First Published in United Kingdom November 2025

First edition November 2025

ISBN 978-1-0369-7306-3

Flying with Fear

My journey across the world

Elizabeth Bond

Dedication

To my husband and daughter, what a great adventure we had in Australia! Lots of love to you both, xo

Acknowledgements

Firstly, my thanks to you, the reader, for choosing my book! I hope that my story of flying with fear will be of some encouragement to you on your journey.

Secondly, huge thanks to my family for all their support and patience with me over the years and for holding my hand on the plane when I needed it!

Lastly, but not least, thanks go to all the wonderful people I have spoken to who have inspired me with their own travel adventures to be brave and spread my wings. I did it!

Contents

Introduction

The purpose of my book is to share the journey I took to manage my fear of flying. I hope by sharing it in writing, it will provide encouragement to anyone trying to overcome their own fear of flying.

Having suffered with flying anxiety for many, many years I write with total understanding of how debilitating and inconvenient a fear of flying can be. I even once off loaded from a plane sitting on tarmac during a thunderstorm at Heathrow airport! (More on that later!) I have also suffered with panic attacks and anxiety and so I understand how hard it can be to face a fear.

I am not a medical professional nor a psychologist, but I have walked the walk and have gone from not flying at all for well over 10 years, to flying halfway around the world and back! I tried a few times to beat the fear before I eventually stopped flying altogether.

It was after a very turbulent flight, that I vowed to myself I would never fly again. Well, you know the saying – never say never!

So what changed? A very special family celebration was motivation for me to get back on a plane. It took small steps, but slowly and surely changes happened and my confidence grew. Starting with a one hour flight 3 years ago, I have recently returned from flying halfway round the world to Australia and back - I did it!

My experience may help you - and I do hope it will - because learning how to manage this fear will open a world of wonderful adventure to you. It will give you the opportunity to explore places that may now seem out of reach when the thought of flying makes you feel physically sick. Overcoming your fear of flying will enable you to meet friends and family living abroad, take holidays and travel to new places. Flying is so much quicker than alternative forms of transport such as road, rail or sailing. It will give you choice but more than that it will also give you confidence when you achieve your goals and see what you are capable of!

If you are reading this, then you have already taken another step, or maybe this is even your first step, to conquering your fear of flying. Put your seatbelt on, sit back and prepare to fly as I describe how I managed to face my fear of flying!

Chapter 1

Where did the fear come from?

For many people flying anxiety can present before they have even taken their first flight. Sensationalist headlines in newspapers and media can contribute to this. For others, it could be the result of an experience during a flight such as turbulence or having an aborted landing. Neither of these would put the plane in any danger, but the experience may be enough to have triggered a fear in the mind of a passenger. Or, it could be that you have been a frequent flyer who has suddenly got scared of being in the air. Whatever the reason behind your fear of flying, there are steps you can take to help you face your fear and I will set out the steps I took.

The first flight I ever took was an Aer Lingus flight from Dublin to Paris. I was about 18 years old and travelled with an older relative.

It was very exciting! I recall being offered a hard boiled sweet from a basket by the air hostess to help pop my ears on take-off!

The engines revved up and as the plane sped down the runway faster and faster it felt as though I was pinned back in my seat until the moment it got lift and soared into the clouds. It does sound wonderful, doesn't it! Many people love that sensation, but not all!

Over the years that followed, I grew to enjoy flying less and less and the thought of flying made me feel physically sick to the point of retching walking to the plane. From dithering over whether to book a flight or not, to wrestling with guilt over letting family down if I didn't and trying to manage anxiety for days or even weeks prior to flying if I did. I totally understand how other fearful flyers feel.

It wasn't until I was on a flight with extremely bad turbulence, travelling alone, that I vowed I would never fly again. Why would I want to take that risk when I could just avoid doing it?

As I mentioned in the Introduction, I once off-loaded a plane stuck on the runway in London due to a thunderstorm. It was my second flight of the day.

All the passengers were boarded ready to depart when the pilot announced that due to the weather conditions we would be delayed. We could hear the storm around us as the rain beat down the windows of the plane. I really had a bad feeling – you know the one, the gut instinct that tells you this is not good. (Don't go!) You think your gut instinct knows best and you start to catastrophise what might happen if you stay on board. Did I really want to fly through a thunderstorm? All the catastrophic outcomes flicked through my mind. I waited anxiously considering what might happen.

Then another passenger asked if they could get off the plane. It was a domino effect! One passenger, then another and another! I could stand it no more and I said I wanted to offload with my family too! The cabin crew let us off. I was very relieved! My anxiety disappeared and was immediately replaced with guilt! However inside the terminal there was chaos due to flight delays and I still had to get a flight home arranged as I was no longer going on to Europe!

Later that day we boarded another plane. The storm had passed - my internal flight touched down safely – except that my family and I were now back home! Our suitcases were goodness knows where! On checking the status of the flight we had offloaded it had arrived safely in Europe. I knew I had let my family down and instead of being in Europe we were right back where we had started from. My gut instinct had been wrong! My fear had lied to me! Fear is often termed False Evidence Appearing Real. This had been a prime example of that!

I am sure many non-flyers are familiar with the effect this

has on family and friends especially if they forego holidays abroad in favour of holidaying at home. Even harder perhaps is if your job depends on you being able to travel at times and you simply can't face flying. It brings with it a level of guilt at letting everyone down, not least yourself, however understanding people may be of your fear.

I am not going to detail my specific anxieties about flying because I will assume that the reader will know full well what they dislike about it and I see no value in adding to anyone else's fears by detailing a list of potential other worries. Worries are for the mind what weeds are in the garden – they can spread and takeover very quickly, starving flowers room for growth. The same it is with those negative thoughts. You latch on to one and another pops into your head and before you know, you are in a downward spiral of fear and catastrophising. Time now to recognise those negative thoughts for what they are and do some weeding!

2010

Chapter 2

Facing My Fear

Realising I had to do something about my fear as I was depriving my family of holidays abroad and limiting my own horizons, I decided to look at ways to beat it, or at the very least, to manage it better.

Fear of Flying Courses

One of the first things I did was to find a fear of flying course.

Many airlines offer these and if you can find one near you I definitely recommend trying this for yourself. The courses often have pilots, engineers and crew who will be there to provide information on the physics and mechanics of flying. There may even be a psychologist on hand to talk specifically about fear of flying.

There will likely be a question and answer session to give you the opportunity to discuss your fears.

I have been on two different courses and they both were very thorough in explaining how aircraft stay in the air, safety procedures, air traffic control, maintenance etc. You may well find that once you have all the noises and bumps and procedures explained to you, your newly gained knowledge will have reassured you that flying is safe. It is because of these courses that I am less concerned now about turbulence, likening it to ‘bumps in the road’. When you are next a passenger in a car or bus, or even a train, close your eyes for a moment or two and feel the sways and bumps along your route. It is similar with air travel, there may be bumps along the way as you travel through the air. Remember too, planes are built to fly!

Keep in mind at fear of flying courses that you will also hear what other people fear about flying, but don't let that put you off. You will come away with a wealth of reassurance and knowledge as the experts answer all the questions you and others put to them.

They will most likely recommend you make your anxiety known to cabin crew when boarding so they can check on you during the flight.

The courses are always well attended because believe me, you are not alone in your fear, so for this reason, I would recommend booking on a course even if you are not intending to fly in the near future, but you feel it is something you might want to do at some point. This is a good way to take the first steps to flying more confidently.

Some courses will also include an 'experience flight' either on the same day as your course or on another date but if you feel you don't want to do this, don't let it put you off attending the seminar sessions.

My first fear of flying course was taken in Dublin and run by a pilot and we had access to an aircraft simulator on which pilots were trained. After learning how much pilots do actually love flying and everyone had asked all their questions about flying, we were allowed in the simulator in pairs. Inside we saw what an aircraft cockpit is like and how pilots fly the plane.

The simulator gave a very real feeling of being in the air. It also provided opportunity to see how things played out in various scenarios and this I felt was beneficial to me because I could ask about situations that were frightening to me and could see procedures for every scenario I brought up. Before long, it feels as though you are in an aircraft and not a simulator at all!

Not all courses offer an aircraft simulator, but they may well offer an actual flight and it is really worthwhile to go on this if they do.

The course instructors usually go along on these experience flights and will explain all the aircraft noises along the way. The course I was on also provided a CD of aircraft noise and a ‘virtual flight’ that I could listen to and this has proved a really helpful tool for me as I use it once a day for a few days before any flight I take.

After I had been in the flight simulator I booked a short one way flight to a nearby city the following weekend.

The flight time was about 35 minutes so that gave me a take off and a short time in the air before landing. I did this with a friend for support.

It was quite scary because this time I knew it wasn't a simulator I was in and I would actually be taking off!

Of course, I was still full of nerves, but I was surer this was something that was safe to do now knowing all the safety procedures and checks that take place. The knowledge that I had gained on the course had been reassuring and having been in the simulator had helped immensely.

I was also armed with a puzzle book, note pad and pen to do mathematics as we had been told keeping the brain occupied would prevent it from thinking negative thoughts. Well, it must have worked for me because I did do the flight!

However, I hadn't been confident enough to book a return flight, so returned via other transport means – and it is alright to do that if you just want to give it a try on a one way trip.

No need to stress yourself more than you need to! One step at a time.

That was my first flight in a very long time under my belt! However, it was to be another decade before I did my next flight and that felt like starting all over again! Years had passed and as anyone with anxiety knows, we are experts at avoidance!

During that decade I went on a second fear of flying course with a major airline. Again, I got good information and reassurance. On this course, the tapping technique known as EFT (Emotional Freedom Therapy) was also used. There was an option for an experience flight too – but I didn't take it! There were handouts however that have been helpful to me to refer back to. The knowledge and reassurance and enthusiasm of those involved in these courses does help to boost your confidence in the aviation industry. It just wasn't the right time for me at that point to do the experience flight.

2022

Motivation

Then came a time when a family event that I very, very much wanted to attend was approaching. So this time I had a very definite motivation for wanting to fly, but I still didn't feel that I could do this easily. I wanted to, I really did. I was determined that I would. Motivation for me played a large part in returning to flying again. It had to be really worth it to make me even consider flying.

It did help that I knew I had enjoyed the flight simulator and I had gained knowledge from the course and the flight with my friend. I also had the further reassurance gained from the second fear of flying course too.

So I made a plan! Perhaps for some it is a need to 'be in control' which lingers behind a flying anxiety, but making this need to be in control into a plan to combat the fear seemed like a good idea to me! Switch it round – don't let fear control you, control the fear instead.

I thought about what my concerns were and what would make me feel happier about flying and came to the conclusion that I needed professional help from a therapist to deal with it. I had done two different fear of flying courses, but still something was holding me back, preventing me from grasping the nettle and booking a flight – or maybe more accurately booking a flight and actually going on it!

Not only had I avoided flying for so long, but I also had allergies and anxieties around that which were magnified by the thought of being in an aircraft cabin flying high in the sky! I knew the course and simulator had helped me take that first short flight, but I hadn't got enough exposure to flying to build on that and this time I felt that one to one therapy was maybe a good route to explore.

I started to watch planes on Flightradar 24 to see how many

flights were in the air, taking off and landing safely each day.

I thought too it would be good to familiarise myself with airports at any chance I got such as leaving family off, or picking them up at airports; sitting in cafes overlooking airports and watching planes come and go.

The main part of my plan though was to seek professional therapy and I got a recommendation for a Cognitive Behavioural Therapist.

Cognitive Behavioural Therapy

So now I had my motivation - the event I wanted to travel to was in London, UK and was an hour and a quarter's flight time from my home. The event was due to take place in September 2022.

In June 2022 I had my first telephone Cognitive Behavioural Therapy session, followed by another each month up until the time of my flight, when I had a call the day before.

I cannot extol how helpful these therapy sessions had been for me in overcoming my fear of flying. I was able to ask all the questions I felt were silly or random about flying and how it made me feel, why I was scared and why I reacted in such a way when others seemingly didn't.

One of the things I learned about myself during Cognitive Behavioural Therapy was I tended not to think beyond the flight. I really couldn't imagine it landing safely and getting off the plane – my mind was stuck in some kind of catastrophic thinking that this would be my last day! That was a bit of an eye opener for me! I was so wrapped up in all my negative thinking of what might happen and what might go wrong – the what if's that are so familiar to people with anxiety – that landing and getting off the plane hadn't registered in my thinking processes.

Once I started to think about the flight landing and concentrating more on what I would be doing when I landed – the purpose of my trip – then I could move beyond the fear and anxiety that was preventing me from flying.

For this reason, I always now plan what I will do when I am at my destination and write up an itinerary that I can look at on the plane. It really did help me!

The benefit of having telephone counselling leading up to my flights also helped quell the nerves and worries that would usually be swirling around my mind in the weeks before my flight. I was doing something positive. I was giving myself a chance to combat this fear – if it worked, it would be great. If it didn't work, well at least I had tried my best.

Alongside my therapy sessions I also tried to practice relaxation techniques. This was beneficial in helping me understand how to relax not just my body but also my mind. This would prove useful on board the plane.

Diet was also something I paid attention to – cutting down on sugar and caffeine intake as I didn't need the nervous energy. Even if you feel it only makes a slight difference, it will still make a contribution to your overall relaxed state.

I also looked into anything known to aid relaxation such as lavender oils, chamomile tea, and some gentle exercise.

So that was my plan!

September 2022 – Facing my Fear

I don't mind admitting I felt very anxious before my upcoming flight, but the therapy sessions had helped me understand what my triggers were and my reactions to those triggers.

I maintained my focus on doing this flight for the sake of my family. I think it's important to say I also wanted to do this for me too – so I could overcome this fear. So, I practiced my relaxation techniques in the days before and I listened to sounds of airplane noises on the CD I had got from the course in Dublin. I tried my best to watch my diet and to get a good walk when possible.

Now I have to admit that even with relaxation techniques I did get a bit stressed the day before my flight.

The stress came to a head during packing! For some reason I was totally confused to the point of tears about whether a cream was a liquid or not! Well, I wasn't a regular flyer and there were security rules and regulations about what can be carried in hand luggage!

Emotions boiled over and tears were shed! I recognise that now as a build-up of stress. Stress can affect us all in different ways and sometimes just a simple thing like that can be the last straw! Being better organised and packing a couple of days earlier might have been a good thing for me to do!

At the airport, we had booked the airport lounge to take away some of the anxieties I had about being in the airport and this provided a quieter space which hopefully would be more relaxing. It was worthwhile doing this, for it really did make a difference for me.

The call came to board the flight and off we went down to

the gate. So far so good! Until that is an announcement was made saying we were delayed and had to return to the departure lounge!

Eventually we got to board and I told cabin crew that I was a nervous flyer. When we were all seated the pilot made an announcement to say that due to a shortage of air traffic controllers in London (it was during the covid era) we would have to wait for a slot. My mind started to have negative thoughts about this – a shortage of air traffic controllers was worrying (I wondered would it be safe to fly) but then my rational brain countered with the fact that we were delayed and waiting and they were only letting in and out what was a safe number of planes. (It was probably safer than ever to fly!)

I could see how easy my mind flitted to negativity when really it was quite a positive thing that we were waiting. It was a clear demonstration that we would not fly unless it was safe to do so. I also believe it was my therapy sessions that helped me have the awareness to recognise the negative thought and to counter it with a more rational one.

We waited 3 hours! Oh my! Sitting on the plane on the tarmac was not what I had wanted or expected would happen! It was time to put my distraction techniques into action.

I knew I couldn't get off in a panic, which did cross my mind to do! So, I took my puzzle book out and did some word puzzles. I played games on a page with pen and paper. I had printed out menus from restaurants we planned to visit and took time over deciding what dishes I might order!

These were things I knew would take my attention off the flight but now I was using them before we had even taken off! You may have other things that would interest you and its worth spending some time on planning how you distract your attention on board if you feel anxious.

After a while, a strange thing happened, I noticed my anxiety went down! All was ok, I was sitting on a plane for 3 hours – ok, I hadn't taken off, I wasn't in the air and I hadn't flown anywhere, but I was still on the plane! All I really wanted now was for the plane to take off! Being on the plane so long, I needed to use the toilet. We were still on the ground, but it still seemed daunting. It didn't help either when I looked in the mirror above the sink and noticed my eyes were very red and bloodshot. Oh no! What was happening to me?! I could feel the anxiety start to take over – would I be ok in the air with red eyes? My family were able to reassure me and moving the air vent from blowing directly on my face I relaxed a little. To this day, however, I bring with me eye drops or put them in my eyes before flying to keep them from getting dry!

Eventually the pilot announced that we now had a slot and were preparing for take-off! I have to admit, by this time I was just relieved that in another hour I'd be able to get off the plane at my destination and I was quite ready to go now! At this point I noticed steam arising around the windows and so I asked cabin crew about this.

They explained what it was and I was reassured it was nothing to worry about. Phew!

Headphones on, hands held with family, the plane sped down the runway and off we went. I did feel anxious during take off, but having listened to aircraft noises on my CD in advance I was familiar with what all the vibrations, whirring and clunking noises were and the expected turns. It does give peace of mind to know a particular noise is the wheels going up, and that the bongs are only for cabin crew to communicate with each other. Eventually the plane reached cruising height, the cabin crew came round with tea and coffees and I switched from my relaxation download and watched a downloaded tv comedy show.

Comedy is good to watch or listen to as it's hard to be anxious when you are chuckling away! Time passed by and we started our descent into London Gatwick. When the plane touched down, I have to admit to a few tears of relief! I had done it!

I hadn't been in London for very many years and the trip was worth the journey many times over!

A few days later and it was time to do the return flight. Having been occupied sightseeing and so on, I hadn't had time to worry about the return flight too much, although it was in the back of my mind.

I was becoming familiar now with the routine of going

through security, getting bags checked, standing in the machine that scans your body and then proceeding to the lounge. This time the plane departed on time, my eyes were sorted (eye drops in) and the plane flew me smoothly home. Goal achieved!

The success of this flight thrilled me! I was delighted to have done this; to have attended my family celebration and to have enjoyed a wonderful few days in London and my family were delighted we all had done this together. We now have many happy memories of that trip.

2023

Chapter 3

Breaking the Fear Habit

Having done a successful flight to London (and back!) my problem now was how did I keep the momentum going and capitalise on my success. After all, for most of us air travel isn't something that we do regularly and as I knew from experience after my first short trip all those years ago, I had a decade of a gap between that and my more recent trip to London. I couldn't let that happen again if I was going to overcome my fear of flying or I would be back at square one.

So, with a determination new to me, nine months later, I had another trip planned, another flight to London!

I put the same plan into action –

- I contacted the Cognitive Behavioural Therapist and booked a series of telephone calls leading up to the date of my flight.
- I practiced relaxation techniques.
- I listened to aircraft sounds from the CD from one of my fear of flying courses.
- A week before my flight I tried my best to cut down on caffeine and sugar (not easy!)
- I had a printed itinerary of all the things I wanted to do and see, to remind myself of why I was flying.

So it was that nine months later I was on my way to London again!

The same preparations were in place – airport lounge was booked – in fact anything that could make the journey easier I did. I made sure my creams and liquids were sorted correctly this time!

The plane went on time and on take off I pulled out my headphones and listened to a relaxation track. After we levelled off at cruising altitude, I relaxed a little and watched some downloads on an ipad. Before I knew, we were commencing descent.

No red eyes this time either!

The return journey was similar and all in all this was a success! My confidence was returning!

2024

Chapter 4

Maintaining the Momentum

As the saying goes, success breeds success!

In 2024 I took two flights! In May of that year I flew to London once more and followed the plan I had set out for my previous trips. I was becoming more and more familiar with going through the airports, going through security and the procedure for boarding. I knew what I was going to do when I found my seat. I had by now also worked out which seat suited me best. Did I want more legroom, an aisle seat or window seat and was front, back or middle of aircraft better.

I found it worth paying for seat selection as it allowed me to be the most comfortable that I could be for the journey.

One thing I found helpful was just blanking my mind from everyone else boarding as people tend to get a bit flustered putting their bags up above their seats and squeezing past each other down the aisle.

Shutting myself off from this hustle and bustle and putting on headphones and music or relaxation downloads really helps alleviate any anxiety whilst waiting for the doors to close prior to take off. Use this time as a chance to settle yourself. You could be the most relaxed person on the plane!

I had also found a Fear of Flying Support Group on a social media platform and this was a very supportive group for people just like me, trying to overcome their flying anxiety. I read how people were facing their fears and while some succeeded and some didn't, either way they were taking steps to move forward, just as I was trying to do. I was inspired by the courage they were showing in facing their fears whether successful or not.

In the Autumn of 2024 I had the opportunity to do a 2-and-a-half-hour flight to Europe. This was a big step up for me! I followed the same procedures and all went well on the outward journey. On the return journey, however, the passenger behind my seat remarked to the air steward that the cabin was very hot.

Oh! Well, that triggered my panic mode! Why was it hot? Was I hot? My anxiety thought then was 'can I breathe?' Well, I wasn't sure. Maybe I couldn't. I know I was fine up to that point, but was I really? Perhaps I wasn't breathing. So it is with anxiety! I had to talk myself down from this with more rational thoughts. I couldn't afford to let myself go full panic! Now was a good time to do some box breathing – a technique taught to me by my cognitive behavioural therapist.

Breathing techniques for anxiety are easily searchable on the internet and box breathing is often recommended. I find it helpful if I can see a square or rectangular shape perhaps on the back of the seat in front of me to focus on whilst doing this technique. Whether the cabin had cooled or not, I don't know, but box breathing and distraction had helped me through this.

It wasn't long until the plane started its descent and for some reason that always calms my mind.

Nonetheless, even with this moment of panic, I had successfully done my first return trip to Europe in many, many years! More memories in the bank!

What I learned from this flight was my triggers could come from any source – something around me, something someone says, something I see. I found it useful to keep my mind focused on the tools that I have learned through therapy and to know when to use them. For this purpose, I also photograph my notes from my therapy sessions so I can read them on my phone and it is so very useful having that to hand.

If you decide to try a form of therapy to help with your flying anxiety, it is worthwhile to make notes to refer back to.

2025

Chapter 5

Flying Across the World

Never in my wildest dreams did I ever imagine that I would travel to Australia – halfway round the world – and back!

In 2025, I did just that! I still find that hard to believe and am amazed that I have gone in the space of 3 years from taking very short flights of just over an hour duration to expanding that to 19 hours flying with only one short stopover of 2 hours.

Motivation is always a big driver and for this trip, like my very first trip to London for that family celebration back in

2022, the motivation was key to doing this journey successfully. I think it's important to say here it wasn't a journey I had planned to do back in 2022 when I took that first flight to London. If I hadn't done that trip and thesubsequent ones, there would have been no way I would have considered taking on such a lengthy journey – two long haul flights – and I would have missed out hugely if I hadn't done this!

What had I learned from my previous trips?

I knew I had flown, I knew I had enjoyed being at my destinations, I knew I could control my anxiety with the right support and tools. But there was still one thing concerning me – I had got panicked about breathing when the passenger behind me on the flight back from Europe had complained about the cabin being hot. If I was going to travel to Australia, I was going to need to be certain I could do such a long flight. There was only one thing for it – I needed to do another flight of similar length to the European flight and see did it happen again. With this in mind, I arranged another trip to Europe again to see how I would manage. It wasn't quite as long a flight as my last journey, but that was ok for me. Again, I had my telephone counselling session and I discussed what my worries and concerns were.

I am happy to say that on this occasion, both flights there and back went well.

Before long, the time came to decide if I was going to accompany my family member to Australia or if I was going to leave her to travel alone.

There were many factors that played into this decision and it wasn't one taken lightly, but I made the commitment to do it and that is what I had to stay focused on.

I had now travelled 3 short return trips within the UK and 2 return trips to Europe. Could I do this? Well, truth be told, I didn't honestly know – but there was only one way to find out. Was I going to let fear control my life, or was I going to control the fear?

The day came when the flight to Australia was being booked. Was I going along too or was I not? It was a great opportunity, would I let it go by? I was determined - I didn't know what lay ahead if I went, but I did know the regret I would feel if I didn't go. My therapist would often point out to me that a ship in port will decay as much as a ship on the high seas – the point being to live your life fully.

The flights were booked! That was it, I was going!

Now, it really wouldn't have helped me one iota to worry about this forthcoming trip for the weeks and weeks that lay ahead before the journey.

So, I put the flying out of my mind for much of the time whilst I got on with everyday activities. Why make each day a misery for weeks on end, when the actual journey itself was only going to be a full day? Only a day. I kept telling myself this – what's a day, all I have to do is sit there, I can do this. There had been occasions when a medical issue meant having to sit for 3 days with my leg resting up, so surely sitting on a plane would be just the same - it was just a matter of reading a book, keeping myself occupied and letting the crew do the worrying. Time passes and the time spent on board a long haul flight would pass too.

One thing I had learned during the months of tackling my fear of flying was not to listen to those people around me that seemed intent on telling me their flying horror stories and undermining my confidence.

It's fair to say people were interested in hearing how I was going to manage a flight to Australia, given that they knew I had a fear of flying! I had to devise a way of deflecting this kind of conversation by quickly changing the subject to something more agreeable for me. Perhaps that was an example of avoidance too, but I acknowledged the comments and quickly diverted the conversation so as not to engage in negativity. I had to maintain my focus and belief that I could do this.

It can happen a lot and I'm sure we all know people who can't wait to recount their nightmarish tales of airports and flying. This really won't help at all because if it is negative, it will feed your anxiety. Instead, I decided I should speak to more people who had travelled afar and enjoyed travel. Their enthusiasm was inspiring! I came to believe if they can do it, then why can't I. Maybe I could too! Looking back, I felt that was quite an important step in my progress and motivation so if, you can, surround yourself with those people who enjoy travel.

Other things I have learned is to pay less and less attention to the headlines that pop up on internet feeds or social media. My advice would be don't click on anything related to flying randomly appearing on your smartphone or device.

Some headlines are harder to avoid on television or radio if an incident does happen and in such circumstances I acknowledged it happened but didn't dwell on it.

There might be all kinds of theories going round, but until proper facts emerge there really is no point stressing yourself out. Leave that to the airline industry to sort!

It's also worth remembering that in all things in life there is a certain element of risk. Nothing is totally risk free. This was something my therapist often reminded me of. Our anxiety and fear wants to protect us but looking for 100% guarantees I would be safe was asking for the impossible.

We take risks every day, driving, as pedestrians, on trains, in everything we do. Flying is just another risk we take. Flying however is regarded as one of the safest forms of transport.

Flying Dublin to Perth, Western Australia

In the weeks leading up to flight day I tried not to dwell on my upcoming journey other than to plan what I needed to pack. This helped me live in the moment and avoid anticipatory anxiety. After all, what good was it going to do me to torture myself with worry and what ifs? With this approach, I enjoyed the build up to the flight by getting on with my everyday routines. I had my plan and was sticking to it. I kept my focus firmly on the prize. Whatever would happen, I would deal with it and that had become my mantra. I will deal with it.

As with everything, time passes and the day arrived. The journey of a lifetime for me was about to begin!

Even at this stage, I was unsure if I could do this journey, but I was as ready as I ever would be. Now it was time to put all my therapy and work to the test. I didn't want to be that ship in port!

I had eaten a good breakfast to keep my blood sugar levels right; I was as prepared as I could be.

I had spoken to my cognitive behavioural therapist a few days before. I had done my relaxation techniques, drank chamomile tea and listened to my flight noise CD from the first fear of flying course.

On arrival at the airport, it was beginning to feel very real. Everything went smoothly through security and on into the lounge area. There were no delays and we boarded the plane. Cabin crew were very pleasant welcoming us on board and I took the opportunity to say I had never flown long haul before. This time I desisted from saying I was nervous, because I was trying to move myself out of that frame of mind. The crew member chatted about my destination and put me at ease. I got all the bits and pieces I would want during the flight out of my case before storing it above the seat in the compartment.

What I wasn't expecting was how smooth take off would be in such a big plane! It really was incredibly smooth. In fact, the whole flight was smooth and I settled in very quickly, headphones on and listening to music and downloads.

On such a long flight there were plenty of meals and drinks

being offered by the cabin crew and this helped pass the time in too.

Before I knew it, the plane was starting its descent and again I was surprised at how smooth the landing was. I had arrived after 8 hours on board! This gave me huge confidence that I could do the second part of the journey which would take just over 11 hours flying time.

With a 2 hour break to change flights, there wasn't a lot of time to get flustered. Bags were checked through and we found our way to the gate for boarding. It's fair to say by this time I was feeling tired.

I was now on board a flight to Perth, Western Australia and ready for take off. Rather than feeling fear, I was starting to feel excited!

Again, take off was a very smooth procedure and once the seatbelt signs were switched off it was time to get settled back into my seat and try to relax.

There were times when the seatbelt signs came back on whenever we encountered turbulence. Once or twice I did feel a bit anxious but I told myself the plane is built to withstand turbulence. I recalled closing my eyes in the car and how turbulence was just like bumps in the road. The crew didn't seem to be panicking about anything.

Other passengers were carrying on resting or watching a film or reading. I said a prayer for our flight and that helped me. Prayer may not be for everyone, but for me it is important and I prayed at various times along the flight path. As the flight went on and the fasten your seatbelt signs went on and off, I realised that this wasn't anything to be concerned about. I reminded myself that planes fly this route daily (I had seen them on Flightradar 24!) and the crew are professionals who know what they are doing. I had to have trust in the professionals.

When I did start to feel nerves kicking in and wanted a further distraction, I put my noise cancelling headphones on and listened to my music playlist which had been carefully selected in advance.

I couldn't help but notice how everyone made their way to the toilets when the seatbelt signs went off and I realised that if the seatbelt signs were on for a long time, then I would be too nervous to get out of my seat to use the toilets so I too started to make my way to the toilets at regular intervals when the signs were off.

That also broke the flight up a bit too, just getting up and walking up and down the aisle – which was always something I was too scared to do on a shorter flight!

When I was in the air 8 hours with 3 hours to go, I felt the countdown to landing was beginning! Imagine that only 3 years earlier a short flight of just over an hour seemed long to me! When it got down to 2hrs 59 minutes, I was delighted to think I'd be getting out of the plane soon - in Australia! I quickly learned not to keep looking at the flight path and the journey time on the screen on the back of the seat because time seemed to pass much more slowly when it was being watched! Time for a movie and I chose a Disney film for something lighthearted and easy to follow.

Before long, the cabin crew were checking all seats were in the upright position and clearing away cups and rubbish and we were preparing to land…in Australia!! How exciting that feeling was! The plane's descent was extremely smooth once again and when we hit the ground I was overjoyed! I truly could not believe I had done it and I think that feeling lasted for several days!

Needless to say, I had a fantastic time in Australia and it was so, so worth the journey!

I still had the return journey to do of course and preparation was also key to that for me too. I had arranged a Whatsapp telephone conversation with the Cognitive Behavioural Therapist scheduled for a few days before I was due to leave.

During that call, he asked me the following question – of all the things I had been worrying about happening, how many of them had actually happened? I had to smile to myself at the other end of the phone because the answer to that was none! Well, that reinforced the message to me that my worries, although powerful enough over the years to keep me from travelling, were absolutely groundless. Another example of FEAR - False Evidence Appearing Real. Now I must add here that it did take a lot of work on myself to get to this point and it took me to find the right support for my needs. What is right for me, may not be right for you, but you will find what suits you best when you are ready to take the next steps to overcoming your fear of flying.

Coming Home

I would like to say that my return flights from Australia were as smooth and easy as the outward journey, but during one of the flights I began to feel the cabin was a bit warm and stuffy and I knew I was going to panic about whether I could breathe or not. So, what did I do to deal with this? I recognised that the warmth had triggered me and I reassured myself that I could breathe. I started the box breathing exercise. This seemed to work and I settled back to listen to my music through my headphones. A little while later, the same thing happened and I did the same box breathing technique. Again, that gave me a great sense of control of being able to stop the panic in its tracks and it is why it is so useful to learn breathing and relaxation techniques in advance so you are able to use them as soon as you feel triggered.

The second flight of my return journey was smooth and by the time we landed back in Dublin, I was tired and ready to go home and had many, many happy memories made with my family.

The big question is would I do this journey again? Yes! Most definitely and I would have so regretted not going.

Chapter 6

Managing Fear

The reason I called this book “Flying with Fear” is because I have come to realise that I will never rid myself of anxiety or fear. Someone asked me after my trip across the world if I was now cured of my fear of flying. I really don’t know the answer to that. Understanding anxiety is something I came to learn about through speaking with my Cognitive Behavioural Therapist. Anxiety is very much there to protect you, we need it to keep us safe in certain situations. I realised my anxiety was like a horse becoming spooked – I needed to calm it down, talk soothingly to myself, take back the reigns of control and face the fears directly. I acknowledged my fears, accepted them, but also firmly focused on what I wanted to do and not what my anxiety was telling me not to do.

It was a difficult thing to do, but with the right support I found my way and felt it possible to manage my anxiety. As I saw progress along the way, my confidence grew.

I sincerely hope that you will find the support and help that will enable you too to achieve your wings and fly with your fear firmly under your control.

Good luck on your journey!

Tips and Techniques

- Relaxation techniques – meditation, tai chi or yoga are good for helping calm the mind and body and are good to practice in advance of your flight.

- Box breathing – this is a useful tool to have in your kit. Information on the correct way to do Box Breathing can be found online. Again, being familiar with the techniques before you go will make it easier to utilise them when you need them.

- Book airport lounges for your flights if you feel a quieter space to sit while you wait to board your flight would be helpful.

- Consider booking speedy boarding if boarding the aircraft first and getting into your seat and settled before everyone else would help you relax.

- Browse the airport shops if this provides a welcome distraction for you.

- Noise Cancelling Headphones are really helpful for blocking out all the aircraft noises.

- Download your favourite music or programmes. Comedy works well, because if you are laughing you are not worrying!

- Bring something with you to distract yourself when you feel anxious, a puzzle book, a coloring book or suchlike.

- Plan your trip – make it as attractive as possible so that you really want to go. Have a list of what you are going to do with you so you can read through this when you feel anxious.

- Checkout events that interest you, restaurants, shows, museums, walks, beaches, sightseeing tours, etc and printout menus and an itinerary to look through whilst on the plane.

- Ensure you have all your items packed correctly for hand luggage, so you aren't stressed when going through security.

- If you decide to take therapy sessions, make sure to take notes so that you can bring them with you to reassure you on your flight. I found photographing them on my phone an easy way to have them readily available.

- Try to avoid engaging in conversations with people intent on relaying horror stories about flying; it will only feed your anxiety. Do speak to people who enjoy travel and are inspiring and encouraging.

- Don’t click on items that pop into your news feed on social media about airline incidents, this also feeds your anxiety.

- Trust in the professionals to do their job well. Your job is to sit back and relax!

- Use your time on board the plane to look through photos on your mobile device as photos often trigger happy memories and are a good distraction.

Finally,

If you have got this far, then thank you so much for reading to the end of my book! I hope you will have found something in it that will inspire or encourage you on your own journey, and that you have many happy flying adventures ahead.

If you have found this book helpful, I would be very grateful if you would leave a review, thank you!

The following few pages contain some images from Australia of the wonderful wildlife and scenery I would have missed out on, had I not faced my fear. I hope this inspires you too.

Figure 1 Kangaroo, Perth, Western Australia

Figure 2 Black Swans, Perth, Western Australia

Figure 3 Beach, Margaret River Region, Western Australia

Figure 4 Sunset over the Indian Ocean, Western Australia

Figure 5 Eucalyptus Tree

Index

Notes

Notes

Notes

Notes

Notes

Notes

Printed in Dunstable, United Kingdom

73498100R00047